A HERMENEUTIC OF LIBERATION

Reading Scripture from the Margins

LEROY BARBER
JESS BIELMAN

A Hermeneutic of Liberation
Written by: Leroy Barber and Jess Bielman

Published by Voices Publishing

Cover design and copy editing
by Casselberry Creative Design

ISBN: 9798375532998

Introduction

The Bible without Liberation

The Bible is a book of freedom. That is what it is designed for and designed to do. If your relationship to the Hebrew Scriptures and the Christian New Testament is not liberating you in the context that you are in, then it has been co-opted by powerful interests. I know the liberative book that I speak of has a sordid past of being misinterpreted, misused as a device for oppression, and taken so far out of its context that it can be hardly recognizable for the brilliant thing that it is – a powerful tool of liberation. But this book perseveres in communities that are inspired by its revolutionary DNA, despite the powers and principalities that mean to use it for their own end.

Many of us who live at the margins of society have been victimized by the bastardization of the Holy Scriptures. We have been keenly aware of how they have been used to oppress women throughout the centuries. Black folks have been tirelessly berated with sickening theological fallacies like the bogus curse of Ham. White supremacy will stop at nothing to flip the scriptures upside down for oppression. In Great Britain and the US in the time of slavery, they went so far as to literally cut out all the liberation passages from the scripture. 90% of Hebrew Scripture was erased because so much of it speaks to freedom under oppression.

More on the Slave Bible

Bible reading has been co-opted. People of color and those from nonwestern traditions know a whole different text, and a whole different way of reading the text. For a lot of white people, their liberation text needs to be liberated. How we interpret the text is a conversation as old as the texts itself. We have seen a history of interpreting these texts in very different perspectives, methods, and ways. The Jewish midrash ways are different from how the New Testament interprets the Hebrew Scriptures. Pre-enlightenment textual analysis is different from the exegetical methods promoted in scholastic models taught in white-serving seminaries that are common today. The approach I offer with humility, understanding this wide history, is a liberation way.

I know a bit of what it is like to read the scriptures from the white scholastic lens. I never used to read the Bible like I do now.

As we venture into this study, the key task will be finding yourself in the story. This first basic principle of interpretation is the cause of so much bad application of the text. We will venture to find ourselves as we investigate the stories for three powerful locators: **culture**, **power**, and **systems**. I have a critique of the way biblical interpretation is taught in the US American and Western contexts of our day. I have learned this critique and better ways of interpretation from my travels and teachers with nonwhite and western perspectives.

Both the Hebrew Scriptures and the Christian New Testament are written in places and times with a multiplicity of cultures, culture clashes, cultural hierarchies, and cultural expressions of faith in God. We see in the scriptures places where pluralism is possible and multiculturalism thrives, and others where culture conflicts drive religious expression. Seeing the way culture is communicated, navigated, and operates is key to finding ourselves in the text. As people of color living in a dominant culture, we see and note the way culture operates naturally in our lives and in the text. Many of us have been enculturated to read culture out of the text. White ideologies will go so far as to suggest that the word of God is "without culture."

We see culture in the ways that privilege is leveraged in the text. The word of God speaks to privilege and culture if we can see it. In this work we will look at Daniel 1 and Acts 6 to see how culture was honored and not honored by those with power.

Common white supremacy hermeneutic does not want to see culture because the myth of God's care operating externally to culture reinforces white dominance. God is a God of liberation in, by, and through culture. Culture is the way we see, communicate, and exist in the world. God does not operate outside of those spaces. God is the creator of those spaces.

Power is another important place to find ourselves in the text. Interpretation steeped in white values will offer the argument that spiritual power is the power that the scriptures point to most often. However, it is clear that the power dynamics that define society and relationships today have existed throughout human history and are spoken to in the scriptures. How power is used, misused, established, and given is a topic of real discovery in the scriptures that we will explore here. We must examine the context of the stories given to us to see where power lies and what is done with it. We can find ourselves in the scriptures as we examine the way power operates.

It is true that there are references to actual spiritual power in the Hebrew Scriptures and the Christian New Testament. However, the presence of spiritual power does not negate the reality that the scriptures teach directly to power as we experience it. Also, when the scripture does speak expressly to spiritual power, most of the time it is utilizing a spiritual power on behalf of the vulnerable who do not have power. We see how power is managed by those who are acting on God's behalf and those who are not. We see power based upon cultural systems like patriarchy and others. The examination of power must be at the center of our interpretation because it is at the center of the gospel (Luke 4:18-19). In a country and a society designed to give one group of people power at the expense of others, we who have been set up for oppression can find the spiritual power in the scriptures to be liberated from the way that power operates in our society.

Finally, we must be mindful when we see systems at play. In many ways, culture, power, and systems interact and express the same basic posture of the Creator towards the people favored by the gospel. The way the scriptures interact with systems is revelatory for those on the margins of the systems of today. We operate within educational, judicial, economic, and other systems designed to benefit some at the expense of others. So did those in the times of these ancient writings. The scripture addresses this directly. We can perk up when we see those anointed by the spirit or directed by God circumventing, dismantling, or speaking truth to those systems. Exploitive systems face unique condemnation in the scriptures, as do those that perpetuate them.

We also see the heart of God in the systems that are created to sustain the communities in which God is invested. We see this in the establishment of the Year of Jubilee, and in the way the apostles set up equity based upon culture and fairness. God creates just and merciful systems and sends prophets into systems that are exploitive and unjust. We find ourselves in those stories as we see, time and time again, God's desire to tear down the systems that keep people of color at the margins.

Chapter 1
Say Their Real Names
Daniel 1 & 3:1-8

Let's start with culture.

Identifying, finding identity in, and living fully into your culture within the context of a white world is a developmental process for most of us that makes us stronger in our sense of self. We often find this self-discovery in the stories of the ancestors, the layers of oppression that we have overcome, and in spiritual beliefs and practices (even as they may conflict with white western Christianity).

The Hebrew people found themselves in a cultural moment in which we can also find ourselves. They were a people that enjoyed the sublime favor of God and also experienced brutal oppression at the hands of their enemies. In Daniel, we pick up the story of God's people moving into exile. It is a culture clash moment when the foundations of the Hebrew culture and identity are tried at the hands of a powerful occupying culture intent on assimilation. While we may not face the premodern oppressive methods, the pattern of the assimilators towards the richness and uniqueness of Hebrew culture may feel a lot like how our culture exists within the US American context.

The book of Daniel starts out:

> [1] In the third year of the reign of Jehoiakim king of Judah, Nebuchadnezzar king of Babylon came to Jerusalem and besieged it. [2] And the Lord gave Jehoiakim king of Judah into his hand, with some of the vessels of the house of God. And he brought them to the land of Shinar, to the house of his god, and placed the vessels in the treasury of his god. [3] Then the king commanded Ashpenaz, his chief eunuch, to bring some of the people of Israel, both of the royal family[a] and of the nobility, [4] youths without blemish, of good appearance and skillful in all wisdom, endowed with knowledge, understanding learning, and competent to stand in the king's palace, and to teach them the literature and language of the Chaldeans. [5] The king assigned them a daily portion of the food that the king ate, and of the wine that he drank. They were to be educated for three years, and at the end of that time they were to stand before the king. 6 Among these were Daniel, Hananiah, Mishael, and Azariah of the tribe of Judah. [7] And the chief of the eunuchs gave them names: Daniel he called Belteshazzar, Hananiah he called Shadrach, Mishael he

called Meshach, and Azariah he called Abednego.

8 But Daniel resolved that he would not defile himself with the king's food, or with the wine that he drank. Therefore he asked the chief of the eunuchs to allow him not to defile himself. 9 And God gave Daniel favor and compassion in the sight of the chief of the eunuchs, 10 and the chief of the eunuchs said to Daniel, "I fear my lord the king, who assigned your food and your drink; for why should he see that you were in worse condition than the youths who are of your own age? So you would endanger my head with the king." 11 Then Daniel said to the steward whom the chief of the eunuchs had assigned over Daniel, Hananiah, Mishael, and Azariah, 12 "Test your servants for ten days; let us be given vegetables to eat and water to drink. 13 Then let our appearance and the appearance of the youths who eat the king's food be observed by you, and deal with your servants according to what you see." 14 So he listened to them in this matter, and tested them for ten days. 15 At the end of ten days it was seen that they were better in appearance and fatter in flesh than all the youths who ate the king's food. 16 So the steward took away their food and the wine

they were to drink, and gave them vegetables.

¹⁷ As for these four youths, God gave them learning and skill in all literature and wisdom, and Daniel had understanding in all visions and dreams. ¹⁸ At the end of the time, when the king had commanded that they should be brought in, the chief of the eunuchs brought them in before Nebuchadnezzar. ¹⁹ And the king spoke with them, and among all of them none was found like Daniel, Hananiah, Mishael, and Azariah. Therefore they stood before the king. ²⁰ And in every matter of wisdom and understanding about which the king inquired of them, he found them ten times better than all the magicians and enchanters that were in all his kingdom. ²¹ And Daniel was there until the first year of King Cyrus.

Finding Ourselves in the Story

This passage addresses some specific ways leaders of color and those from oppressed communities live under oppressed systems every day. Dominant culture using violence for oppression and assimilation is apparently as old as our ability to document stories. Our task is to find ourselves and our communities in these stories. Though the text indicates God had given over Israel into the hands of Babylon, God was still on the side of his people.

Black liberation theologian James Cone gives us a road map for a plain interpretation of the text. He says, "God is on the side of the oppressed, God has made the choices, you cannot be on the side of the oppressed and the oppressor." It is clear, though God may have allowed Babylon temporary temporal power, God is on the side of Daniel, Hananiah, Mishael, and Azariah and the Hebrew people.

One of the dangers of the common white supremacy hermeneutic is its ability to get us to align with the oppressor in the stories. We will see this later in some of Jesus' parables. Our job is to look for culture, power, and systems. Israel lost the war and is now the property of Babylon. This sets up the Hebrew people as the nondominant culture. It sets up a power structure leaving them at the mercy of another culture. If we look closer, we will see the system at work. We identify with Daniel, Hananiah, Mishael, and Azariah and the Hebrew culture as people of color in a culture dominated by white values, white perspectives, and white agendas. This sets up a culture of whiteness that uses power to promote its interests at the expense of ours. We are Daniel, Hananiah, Mishael, and Azariah and the kingdom of Babylon is the US American and western worldview, laws and systems, and cultural norms.

Assimilation - What is in a Name?

Just as whiteness sets up systems to advance its own agenda, Babylon did as well. The king could not oppress the people as effectively as possible without leaders, so Daniel and his friends were forced to be tools to oppress their own people. To do this, Babylon had to select and train them in the Babylonian way. They wanted the best Hebrew talent to be assimilated into their culture. By so doing, they would use their leadership to promote the empire. Babylon needed these leaders to help get their message and agenda to the people. They needed leaders from Israel to instruct the Hebrew people in the ways of their new dominant culture.

We have seen this across time. Europeans needed Africans enculturated into slavery culture to make the slave trade continue. European myths that claim slavery existed widely in Africa before European invasion have been proven to be historically false. Europeans, like Babylon, needed to choose the strongest and best to make their agenda a reality. We also see this enculturation pressure today as we see white America in overt and subtle ways insist others learn English if they want to thrive in this land.

This passage gives us some clues as to how to lead when your community is in bondage. Oppressed communities need unassimilated leaders to exist within oppressive patterns. In our time, these oppressive patterns look like black and brown men and women being arrested at disproportionately high rates, women commonly paid less for equal work across a myriad of industries, Black women attacked for their hair, and Asian hate has also come to the forefront in the Covid era. As people of color, we need unassimilated leaders to lead us as we navigate these assaults on our bodies and culture.

I understand the pressure to want to just assimilate. It is the path to most comfort. Some of us resort to, "I am going to just get paid and live my best life." I am a black man with a doctorate and 30 years of experience doing community and justice work. All this labor does not give me a reason to sit back and just enjoy comforts. All this fuels my responsibility to lead. Daniel, Hananiah, Mishael, and Azariah had a potential easy pathway: assimilate, lead on behalf of the new cultural norms and values that would oppress their people, and forget the old ways of their own culture. But God's call was to the well-being and the sustaining of the Hebrew culture for the Hebrew people.

The king could teach a master class today on forced

assimilation. He even took a little bit of culture from the Hebrew temple with him when he sacked the city. He did that to bring a small amount of comfort to their oppressed situation. We see this today also. Students at predominantly white colleges will find that there may be soul food night at the cafeteria, yet little support for their Black Student Union or institutional support when they expose racism in the classroom. So often white communities will want to engage culture on the levels of celebrating food and entertainment, but never engage cultural uniqueness and the stories of suffering distinctive to cultural forms. They want Hawaiian luaus but not a full exploration of colonization on native Hawaiian lives, culture, and land. The king grabs some things from the temple, but certainly does not want authentic Hebrew culture to exist in his land. He is looking to satisfy a surface level engagement with the Hebrew past and religious expression.

The king had some specific criteria for selection of leaders because he knew he wanted to assimilate the strongest leaders amongst the people. Power structures will always fall back on assimilating those they see that have the most "potential" according to their convictions and ideals. In our case, whiteness likes people of color with not too much cultural distinctiveness but also are clearly nice, well-dressed, strong, articulate, etc. They want to assimilate the best of the best as defined by not too much deviation from whiteness itself.

The king's agenda was not to keep the Hebrew culture but to expand Babylonian culture, and he took a significant step in that direction by changing the names of the Hebrew leaders Daniel, Hananiah, Mishael, and Azariah. They became Belteshazzar, Shadrach, Meshach, and Abednego. Changing their names changed their ethnic identity. It stripped away the ability for them to be referenced as who they were... Hebrews. How many of us have had to change our name to make us more palatable for US white culture? I know fellow black brothers and sisters that have worked alongside white people for years who still do not get their names correct. Asian adoptees sacrifice the pronunciation of their names. Latinx folks compromise the beautiful accents of their native language to enter white spaces. Dating back to even European immigration, immigrants have chosen more Americanized names to fit into culture as a way of survival.

The colonizer agenda is assimilation. So Daniel, Hananiah, Mishael, and Azariah had to change their names. When you change your name to accommodate another culture, your history is often vanquished. The history of the new culture becomes your history. As black folks we are expected to make the history of the

US our history. Fredrick Douglass reminded us that the US independence of the colonies is not our history in his 4th of July address entitled "What is the 4th of July to a Slave." He argued that US American history is a celebration for white folks and a day to memorialize dehumanizing tragedy for black folks.

Assimilation goes beyond naming. A friend once summed up assimilation in the workplace by saying, "Many organizations recruit for diversity but onboard for conformity." Make no mistake, my BIPOC friends: colleges, organizations, corporations, and government agencies are coming for you. They want the diversity that you bring that will show up on spreadsheets. They want to offer you scholarships and hire you, but they are expecting you to assimilate. They want your representation but not the change you bring.

Ultimately these white settings end up demanding that you make the white psyche your norm. Whiteness wants you to measure your culture through their own patterns, customs, and rituals. We see this all the time. There is food and "ethnic" food. There are hair products and "ethnic" hair products. White is the norm, and variation to white is not.

I work with leaders of color all the time who are navigating the real temptation to assimilate and find their value in white values. For those who have grown up in disinvested economic communities, assimilation can provide an avenue to "get out." I have heard the logic over and over that if I get out, I can make change and come back. While few do, I see some people who fall prey to the enticement that Daniel, Hananiah, Mishael, and Azariah did not. "The king chose me." Being found worthy of white choosing can be so inviting. Psychologists refer to this as internalized racism. We can come to believe that whiteness is indeed superior and that being chosen by whiteness gives us a greater sense of value and worth.

The king needed Babylonian values to be learned so that the Hebrew values could be unlearned. Linda Tuhiwai Smith, a professor of indigenous education at the University of Waikato in Hamilton, New Zealand, says of the way colonization exists in her country, "The colonizer did not simply design an education system. They designed an education especially to destroy indigenous cultures, value systems and appearance." This was the same for the Hebrew culture under Babylonian rule as it is now for the US American context.

We see this in the story because it is not enough that these leaders lived authentically into their culture in service to Babylon. They did and were successful.

But as the story unfolds, their rise to power brought a backlash from the assimilation agenda. Even as they helped the king, the forces for assimilation were more interested in killing Hebrew culture than even the success of their crown.

What is most striking about this story is that it is told most often from the perspective of colonization. Western Christianity is a cultural form of the faith that is so twisted with the ideas of a colonized worldview. The common retelling of this story shows how often we cannot even see when the values are at work. The main characters' names are Daniel, Hananiah, Mishael, and Azariah. These are their names given from their Hebrew culture as people of God's promise. Yet in every Sunday school class and sermon I have ever heard, no one uses their real names. Everyone uses their colonized names – Shadrach, Meshach, and Abednego. Worse still, this is a common story told to children with catchy songs sung to help kids remember.

What are we teaching the children? There is a path to being faithful to God in the colonizing way of the world. This is a false gospel.

Our Culture is Our Strength

Next, Daniel mounts a protest so that he and his

companions can stay true to their culture by way of their diets. This is not that unusual. For so many, food is an extension of culture. It is the space in which community happens and culture distinctiveness can be tasted. Daniel, Hananiah, Mishael, and Azariah wanted to stay true to what empowered their leadership, namely the nurturing and growth that they experienced in the womb of their culture. They were leaders in Jerusalem before they were selected as leaders in Babylon.

So many of us were leaders in our communities before we started working in white spaces. Before that job or university came knocking, we were leaders within the values and frameworks of our families, neighborhoods, and churches. It can be a fight for us to stick to the convictions and values that were instilled in us when we are asked to lead in white spaces. Often a rejection of white cultural norms is interpreted as a lack of competence, not being a team player, or simply not fitting in to the organizational mission. I have seen these dog whistles over and over.

Daniel, Hananiah, Mishael, and Azariah rejected the assimilated culture but "learned the king's ways." This is a valuable distinction. As people of color, we have intrinsically learned how to be aware of dominant culture. We are skilled in multicultural dynamics and communication because we live it every day. Learning the king's ways is essential to not acquiescing to the king's ways. They were wise in the oppressive context. We know this. Today we call it code switching. Code switching is a burden put on people of color who can communicate within their culture in particular ways that they cannot in environments shaped by and for white people. Daniel, Hananiah, Mishael, and Azariah were doing the code switching of their day. For them, that was navigating all the new requirements put on them through their new vassal state relationship with Babylon while keeping to their vegetarian diet.

The next step in the king's masterclass on oppression was control through fear. When all else fails, those in power have the option of bending others to their will through the threat of exercising their control in ways that are harmful to you. Police through use of force, employers though threat of termination, teachers through the power of grading, or politicians through the creation of policy. It may get more sophisticated in some circles, but power uses power to keep power. No doubt Daniel, Hananiah, Mishael, and Azariah were probably scared at times. Most leaders of color that I know show great courage in the face of those that try to control them. We teach young leaders of color about their power and identity so that when (not if) they are faced with the controlling interests of white culture, they have a solid leg of identity to stand on.

The story indicates that the official showed favor and allowed the four to keep their diets under the agreement that it would not impact their work for the Babylonian kingdom. The text has an important detail - God caused the official to show favor. Even though they were no longer in the promised land, God continued to be invested in his people. This is because God continues to show favor to oppressed people who are tasked with preserving their life and culture in the face of subjugation. God has chosen a side in the struggle of oppressors and the oppressed. In this story, God does the important work of mystically manipulating the official so that the oppressed could continue to draw strength from their culture in this most crucial time.

We learn through those that have practiced the faith before us that when God wills something, watch it work. In this case Daniel, Hananiah, Mishael, and Azariah are thriving by staying true to their culture, learning but not acquiescing to the king's ways, and most importantly continuing to seek God. Therefore, they became the king's choice. The king must have naively thought that his systematic assimilation was working. It is clear by his later ire that he attributed the success of the four to his subjugation of them. He commanded others to follow Daniel, Hananiah, Mishael, and Azariah's ways. They were put in positions of power and created a multicultural environment for Hebrews to keep their cultural diet and help Babylonians be better themselves. Everyone was better by the four exercising their culture in their way.

The takeaway is that this world needs leaders of color. The world needs our nuance, our commitment to community, our style. We need to be in places of leadership in business, politics, education, arts, and faith. Not simply to do diversity, equity, and inclusion work, but in the highest-level jobs that set the entire culture of equity in the organization or institution. However, when this happens, we can get blowback from our community. Some must have seen Daniel, Hananiah, Mishael, and Azariah and thought they sold out. I am sure their friends and neighbors under the same oppression assumed that the path of assimilation got the four to their high place. Knowledge of empire does not make you a traitor or not legit. We use that knowledge of the empire to, like Daniel, Hananiah, Mishael, and Azariah, subvert the empire.

We are made, wired, and empowered by the God of the Hebrew exiles to lead as our truest unassimilated selves. This is the leadership the world needs. God is ready for us to walk in our leadership as inequity surrounds us and our communities. There is an often-quoted poem from Marianne Williamson that captures this dynamic. She says, "Our deepest fear is not that we are inadequate. Our deepest fear is that we are powerful beyond measure." She goes on to say, "Our playing small does not serve the world." God is on the side of the oppressed and is raising up leaders from these spaces to transform societies.

The Backlash When Living into your Culture in Assimilation Spaces

8 Therefore at that time certain Chaldeans came forward and maliciously accused the Jews. 9 They declared[b] to King Nebuchadnezzar, "O king, live forever! 10 You, O king, have made a decree, that every man who hears the sound of the horn, pipe, lyre, trigon, harp, bagpipe, and every kind of music, shall fall down and worship the golden image. 11 And whoever does not fall down and worship shall be cast into a burning fiery furnace. 12 There are certain Jews whom you have appointed over the affairs of the province of Babylon: Shadrach, Meshach, and Abednego. These men, O king, pay no attention to you; they do not serve your gods or worship the golden image that you have set

up."

[13] Then Nebuchadnezzar in furious rage
commanded that Shadrach, Meshach, and
Abednego be brought. So they brought these
men before the king. [14] Nebuchadnezzar
answered and said to them, "Is it true, O
Shadrach, Meshach, and Abednego, that you
do not serve my gods or worship the golden
image that I have set up? [15] Now if you are
ready when you hear the sound of the horn,
pipe, lyre, trigon, harp, bagpipe, and every
kind of music, to fall down and worship the
image that I have made, well and good.[c] But
if you do not worship, you shall immediately
be cast into a burning fiery furnace. And who
is the god who will deliver you out of my
hands?"

[16] Shadrach, Meshach, and Abednego
answered and said to the king, "O
Nebuchadnezzar, we have no need to answer
you in this matter. [17] If this be so, our God
whom we serve is able to deliver us from the
burning fiery furnace, and he will deliver us
out of your hand, O king.[d] [18] But if not, be it
known to you, O king, that we will not serve
your gods or worship the golden image that
you have set up."

Naturally the success of Daniel, Hananiah, Mishael, and Azariah brought about powerful enemies. Unassimilated people of color will always pose a threat to the establishments that look to keep the status quo as a way of serving the powerful. These forces are powerful. In this text they made laws against the uniqueness of the Hebrew culture. The mandate was clear: assimilate or succumb to the threat of physical violence. US American minorities that have fought to establish their own rights have seen this time and time again. If you do not accept the lower status and even feel grateful for the opportunity to be in this society, then you deserve the violence of the state that is preserving society's purity.

We make laws to keep assimilation in order.

The only option is to stand up to power.

Daniel, Hananiah, Mishael, and Azariah stood up to power and stood on the God of their culture. The king's attitude towards them changed drastically when they stood up to the control of the state. Nothing can be more offensive to those with absolute power than the insistence that their power has limitations and there is something higher than them. We see this in smaller ways in our leadership journey. When the threat of losing the job is gone, we find a freedom from the loyalties that institutions ask us to have, even as they are not going to be loyal to us. Standing up to power means the release of how we benefit from that power. The brilliance of the Montgomery bus boycott was the incredible resilience of the boycotters to remove their own lives from the benefits that the bus offered them. They had power when they began meeting their own transportation needs outside of the unjust system that assumed their dependance.

Standing up to power can be both invigorating and lonely. Not all people who mount incredible fights succeed in the ways that Daniel, Hananiah, Mishael, and Azariah or the bus boycotters succeeded. These four had faith in God that did not waver under the threat of those with earthly powers. Their brilliant response when asked to worship the gods of their oppressors showed the deep impact of their unassimilated convictions. Their response was first to reiterate their history and culture. This was a reminder both to themselves and the oppressor before them. Their faith had an address and practical ways that God had been with them. Because God was faithful in the past, God could be faithful in the future. So their response was "God will save us; even if he doesn't, our God has done enough already."

This rejection of the oppressor's power for something

higher defeats the whole system of assimilated oppression. For those with power it is not good enough to just serve the agenda of power, they want us to turn away from the power we have that is found in our identity, history, and culture. Look at what is sending the colonizing enterprise into a rage today. Critical race theory is a way of honestly looking at history and culture that was until recently only a source or conversation in graduate sociology spaces. It affirms that race is a social construct and a dominant way that society is organized. It has become some mysterious evil to those who benefit from oppression because they do not want history to be told accurately.

Why does the colonizing enterprise not want you to know who you are and where you came from? Why do they not want other people to know who you are and where you came from?

We can answer this question sociologically or psychologically, but I want to think about it theologically. Maybe it is because we know that God has always shown up on the side of the oppressed.

There is a spirit of resistance over 400 years and another 150 years of Jim Crow through which we can trace the movements of God's people. God's presence is the freeing of oppressed people. Like the King of

Babylon, this is the message of God that they do not want out in the air. Theologically, the king and the oppressive ways of government or economic interests today do not want the poor to have hope. Resistance movements are built upon hope.

This is what the gospel does, this is what the gospel is. The story of God for us, from us, to the whole world. These are stories of our triumph in the midst of the historical fiery furnaces of people of color all over the globe.

The Story of God to the Barbers

My great grandmother was a domestic worker in a white household. Domestic workers were a holdover structure from slave times. We know that slavery did not go away. It simply adapted after the Emancipation Proclamation. My grandmother would tell us a story about her mother, my great grandmother.

My great grandmother was raped by a slave master. This rape resulted in the birth of a child. As was common, that child, carried and birthed by my grandmother, was sold into slavery by the man that raped her. With her own child birthed from her body taken and sold, she was forced to go into the house of this man and care for his other children. It was her job to make sure these children were fed, changed, rocked, and put to sleep. I cannot dwell on this too much without profound sadness and anger. I wonder how many nights my great grandmother held the babies of her oppressor, wishing she could hold hers. She had no recourse but prayer, to cry out to God in ways only a mother's heart can.

That is profound grace. That is profound strength. Her ability to care for the children of her oppressor shows an internal fortitude and spiritual strength that is alive in my body and flows in the veins of my children. This can only be accomplished by the same God who saved Hananiah, Mishael, and Azariah from the furnace. The God who we know has made the choice to be on the side of the oppressed in the struggle for justice.

We sit in the privilege of knowing the Creator and God of the oppressed because that kind of faithfulness, heartbreak, and grace ushered God into our lives. It is in our DNA as people living in a land, under a government, and in a society that debates whether black lives ever really matter. This is the gospel they want hidden from us that they cannot tap into, but we can. In my blood runs the generations of singing praise to God, moaning their way through it from heartbreak. I am their legacy.

Chapter 2
The First Miracle
John 2:1-12

On the third day there was a marriage at Cana
in Galilee, and the mother of Jesus was there;
[2] Jesus also was invited to the marriage, with
his disciples. [3] When the wine gave out, the
mother of Jesus said to him, "They have no
wine." [4] And Jesus said to her, "O woman,
what have you to do with me? My hour has
not yet come." [5] His mother said to the
servants, "Do whatever he tells you." [6] Now
six stone jars were standing there, for the
Jewish rites of purification, each holding
twenty or thirty gallons. [7] Jesus said to them,
"Fill the jars with water." And they filled
them up to the brim. [8] He said to them, "Now
draw some out, and take it to the steward of
the feast." So they took it. [9] When the steward
of the feast tasted the water now become
wine, and did not know where it came from
(though the servants who had drawn the water
knew), the steward of the feast called the
bridegroom [10] and said to him, "Every man
serves the good wine first; and when men
have drunk freely, then the poor wine; but you
have kept the good wine until now." [11] This,
the first of his signs, Jesus did at Cana in

Galilee, and manifested his glory; and his
disciples believed in him.

¹² After this he went down to Caper'na-um,
with his mother and his brothers and his
disciples; and there they stayed for a few days.

Looking for Power

If the key to unlocking the story of Daniel 1 is our
ability to look for culture, then the key to opening
up the story commonly referred to as the First Miracle
is to look for power.

This is a story that happens in everyday life. It is not a
high and holy event. Though the union of marriage is
seen as sacred, Jesus is not doing his first miracle in
an expressly religious space. It is the wedding of
families that had some means and wealth. We see a
power hierarchy. There is the bridegroom and the
family hosting, there are guests, there are servants,
and there is a steward who would oversee the
servants. The bridegroom does not need to interact
directly with servants because the steward is hired for
their management. Jesus' family is among the guests
to the party and would have been shown all the proper
formalities as such.

The major conflict in the tale is that the wine runs

out. It would have been the steward's job to secure enough wine for the servants to properly dole out the right wines at the right times. No doubt the absence of wine at this moment in the party would have been an embarrassment to the master, with consequences for the steward and servants. The steward is a working-class person whose job is on the line in this situation.

As the wine runs out, the steward must have had a relationship with Mary because she calls upon her son to solve his problem. The steward didn't know the difference in the wines; all he knew was that the wine was good. Jesus solves the man's problem even though he does not know what or how it happened.

First, Jesus objects when his mother approaches him, telling her that it is not time. But it is his mom, so… Jesus engages the servants in a preposterous idea. Think about what is on the line for everyone if they run water out to this wedding and say that it is wine. Everyone up the power chain is embarrassed. The bridegroom is embarrassed that he not only ran out of wine, but in turn gave water to the guests. The steward loses his livelihood, and the servants will probably ultimately be blamed, because that is how power works.

Jesus' first miracle is keeping those without power

from being blamed for something they did not do.

What is the Miracle?

Let's look at the miraculous moment. The miracle
happens between the filling of the jars and the serving
of the drink. The liquid goes in as water and comes
out as wine. The key to understanding this story is to
look closely at not only who this miracle was for but
who even knows about it. The bridegroom and the
guests are surprised that the best wine wasn't served
first. They do not know where the wine came from.
The text indicated that the steward didn't know. In the
translation we used here, the point of the story comes
in the parenthetical:

(though the servants who had drawn the water knew)

The only people who knew about the miracle were
Jesus and the servants. Jesus' mom probably figured
it out, too. Tradition tells us that this is the first
miracle. If that is the case, these servants were the
first people other than Jesus' family to know what his
abilities were. The savior of the world has come, and
he lives 30 years before his ministry begins. As he is
coming out to the world, the first people to know are
servants.

He could have made a big show of the event. He

could have overshadowed the wedding and performed a wedding trick that would have turned the evening on its head. Instead, he rolls out back, with his working-class folks, and turns water into wine.

Let's pay attention to power. Seeing culture, power, and systems is a key to interpreting the Bible from its liberative vantage point. Jesus is intentional to do this in the presence of the servants. He is intentional to keep it from the bridegroom and the guests. From its inception this gospel has never been for the powerful; it is at its core looking to overturn the systems of power that create servants and guests. Jesus doesn't duck into the back to hide. Jesus ducks in the back to bless those he came to serve, lift up, and die for.

Jesus, in this passage, is serving the servants. No one lost their jobs, no one took the wrath for the powerful covering a mistake. John is very careful to write the story to this end as well. John wants the reader to understand who knew about the miracle and who didn't.

From this point in the story of Jesus' life, he is very popular and rarely alone. Jesus shows up to places and there are crowds. Where would these crowds have come from? Who were these crowds? What did the crowds hear or know that inspired them to show up everywhere he went?

The wedding guests did not go back to their homes and tell everyone about the miracle because they did not know. The bridegroom did not trumpet the miracle that happened at his wedding. He just drank the good wine second and probably did not think about it again.

Those crowds are produced by marginalized folks. The streets speak. They did in their time like they do in ours. Marginalized communities often have relational communication networks that include our aunties, cousins, and neighbors. I can imagine the conversation back in the hood:

"Sis, I was working the Smith family wedding last night. Yo, the wine ran out and ohhh I thought, here we go again, these rich folks gonna blame us and the boss. But this dude Jesus showed up and told us to pour the water into the wine barrels."

"No way!"

"But I thought, what the hell, we gettin' bounced from this job anyway."

"I swear to you, sis, that water became wine… damn good wine, too. I had a drink or two."

"I think he is the prophet. Ya, seriously."

From this point in the story those on the fringes are those that are gathered to him. This is the way of his entire ministry after this. Those on the margins get Jesus, pursue Jesus, and are transformed by Jesus. The elites fight with Jesus, try to discredit Jesus, and ultimately kill Jesus. The end of the narrative unit says that "his disciples believed." Who are these disciples? They are not the formally educated rabbinic students of the rabbi class. These are fishermen, tax collectors, and other working-class folks. I wonder if there were not a couple of wedding workers in the twelve.

The marginalized folks are convinced of who Jesus is, and over and over go out to see him. They make up the bulk of his work and ministry. Without them, Jesus' popularity and message does not and cannot move throughout the area and ultimately change the world. Imagine had Jesus chosen the powerful to be the messengers for his Good News. He would have had to make formal presentations before the counsels, received oversight and accountability from a committee, and had to toe company lines with his critics. Jesus was not about all that. He turned to where the action is.

The work of Jesus gets pushed out into the world

through marginalized folks. God made a choice: the savior of the world would be close to the marginalized who could bring change from the bottom. There was little resistance to the Good News amongst those that could most benefit from it. They were not put off by his threatening of the status quo. They had everything to gain from the reality of a kingdom that was meant to bring up those on the margins and take down those with power.

This story is a microcosm of the gospel itself. Something miraculous has happened, everyone benefits from it, only the servants know the truth, and the powerful are left out of understanding the transformation that has happened. This was the gospel in that moment; it was the gospel Jesus brought, and it is the gospel that still transforms today. We must see power at play to read the scriptures, to see the gospel.

Of course, this is flipped upside down from how the white western US American version of Christianity operates. In the US, it is wealthy and connected people who take the gospel to the poor because they "need it." Untold resources have been spent on white US American Christians going into other countries to bring the good news. As if the bridegroom has anything to say to the servants about how the best wine got served. A little bit of the religion of Jesus combined with wealth and privilege is a dangerous combination.

This Gospel in Action

These servants exercised faith in Jesus by putting water in the jars and having the audacity to serve it. They exercised the faith that Jesus calls so many to in the gospels. Their faith brought about change for the entire party. Jesus brought good to all through the faith of the servants. There is a world beneath the power structures that these servants existed within. It is a world that the powerful does not know and cannot see. Their world and Jesus' influence connected, and the magic of the gospel came to life.

This should have incredible implications on our understanding of the gospel and how it is presented to marginalized communities. The powerful have chosen themselves as those with stewardship over the gospel. This is a choice from human wisdom, not God's wisdom. The powerful have created a gospel that centers them, suits their agenda, and have created entire systems of interpreting the scriptures to undergird their way of dancing around a gospel that was given to the servants.

God has put leadership into the oppressed, not the wealthy. The message that heals the world is in the hands of the oppressed. We do not have to conform to the patterns of a white world to be effective with and for the gospel. We do not need to assimilate to the churches, denominations, and nonprofit organizations largely run by white people who want to do good in underdeveloped countries or US American abandoned communities. There is little to no leadership they can offer to us in these spaces. We have seen how the wine is made. We know the secret is not given to the bridegroom and his guests.

God has given us a message and a culture that is for the healing of the nations. Everyone at the party got to enjoy the wine, but it was provided by Jesus and the servants. The nations have the opportunity for healing from the gospel as it comes from where God has intended it - from the marginalized. We have seen the destruction of human lives and entire civilizations when the powerful claim their actions are from the authority of the gospel. The crusades, colonization, and slavery were all completely antithetical to the way of God but claimed to be inspired by the tenets of Christianity. The powerful can only bastardize the faith. The servants create good for all. We must see how power works in interpreting the scriptures or we lose so much of where and what the good news is.

Christian theologian James Cone does an excellent job at analyzing the gospel as it looks particularly at the US American experience and history. For him, black people are the people that God has chosen. God is specifically working through black people, black culture, and for black liberation. This is because the US has a past, present, and future of oppressing its black citizens. When people are oppressed, the good news is that God is working on their behalf. Part of that good news is God's commitment to then bring down those who are powerful.

God's agenda is to reveal himself to the oppressed and through the oppressed. Colonization works to keep one group above the other. These agendas will always be at odds with one another. The work of God is the undoing of systems of power that exist to keep people oppressed. This is not only for those that already belong to the church. It is the way God operates in the world. God gives significant voice to the outcast.

God is raising up those from marginalized backgrounds to be teachers. The margins are where leaders are coming from and setting the tone for the kingdom in our time. We are setting the tone and agenda for what God is wanting to do in the world.

This should change everything about the gospel - how we serve, how we do missions, how we read the scripture, how we educate. We see power used illegitimately so often. This happens when we see a room full of men deciding what women can or cannot do. A room full of government officials and concerned citizens meeting about homelessness but with no people experiencing homelessness there to lead them. We see rooms full of white people creating programs for people of color. The height of arrogance is a room full of people who think they know better for others than they know about themselves. This has been the way the gospel has been used for too long.

85% of the $300 million given out to nonprofit organizations each year is given to organizations led by white people who are doing work in communities of color. There is no way this can bring about the gospel. Dominant culture will come back with over-spiritualized answers to avoid accountability from the gospel. Jesus brings back people's humanity repeatedly. He releases all his power at one wedding feast, looking at servants and saying, "I am going to give you something that the wealthy folks upstairs don't know; they are going to marvel, but you know the story." And of course the word spreads, stories are told, crowds gather, and the powerful are left out.

There are ways in a culture group that stories are uniquely spread. "Jesus did some shit." This is how the gospel spreads when marginalized folks start talking. This is not the western "rules" approach to the gospel. And as we will see, when rules and systems start to dictate the way that the people can operate, Jesus takes those down. We have seen how to look for culture in Daniel 1, we have seen how to look for power in John 3, next let's examine how to find systems in the scripture. As we build this foundation, we will see the liberative aspects of the scriptures come alive.

Chapter 3
Parable
Luke 19:11-27

The Parable of the Ten Minas

11 While they were listening to this, he went on to tell them a parable, because he was near Jerusalem and the people thought that the kingdom of God was going to appear at once. **12** He said: "A man of noble birth went to a distant country to have himself appointed king and then to return. **13** So he called ten of his servants and gave them ten minas.[a] 'Put this money to work,' he said, 'until I come back.'

14 "But his subjects hated him and sent a delegation after him to say, 'We don't want this man to be our king.'

15 "He was made king, however, and returned home. Then he sent for the servants to whom he had given the money, in order to find out what they had gained with it.

16 "The first one came and said, 'Sir, your mina has earned ten more.'

17 "'Well done, my good servant!' his master replied. 'Because you have been trustworthy in a very small matter, take charge of ten cities.'

¹⁸ "The second came and said, 'Sir, your mina has earned five more.'

¹⁹ "His master answered, 'You take charge of five cities.'

²⁰ "Then another servant came and said, 'Sir, here is your mina; I have kept it laid away in a piece of cloth. ²¹ I was afraid of you, because you are a hard man. You take out what you did not put in and reap what you did not sow.'

²² "His master replied, 'I will judge you by your own words, you wicked servant! You knew, did you, that I am a hard man, taking out what I did not put in, and reaping what I did not sow? ²³ Why then didn't you put my money on deposit, so that when I came back, I could have collected it with interest?'

²⁴ "Then he said to those standing by, 'Take his mina away from him and give it to the one who has ten minas.'

²⁵ "'Sir,' they said, 'he already has ten!'

²⁶ "He replied, 'I tell you that to everyone who has, more will be given, but as for the one who has nothing, even what they have will be taken away. ²⁷ But those enemies of mine who did not want me to be king over them—bring

them here and kill them in front of me.'"

I am grateful to René August and Jonathan Brooks for my thinking on this text. I saw Jonathan break down this passage at the 2021 Christian Community Development Association Conference morning bible study. He credited René who opened his eyes up to seeing this passage the right way.

Prior to this passage is the story of a tax collector named Zacchaeus, who most of us know as a short guy who wanted to see Jesus, so he climbed a tree. However, the most notable aspect of the story is not his physical stature or the lengths he went to in order to get a look at Jesus. Jesus meets with Zacchaeus, to the dismay of those in the crowd that do not like the way tax collectors utilize a system to exploit people for their own financial gains.

Zacchaeus's response to meeting Jesus is declaring that he will give half of his possessions away and give back any money that he cheated others out of. In essence Zacchaeus rejects the system that made him wealthy at the expense of others. The gospel writers often use parables to teach a lesson about the stories that directly precede them. This is no different. Jesus' response to Zacchaeus' new commitment is, "Today salvation has come to this house, because this man, too, is a son of Abraham. For the Son of Man came to

seek and to save the lost." (Luke 19:9-10)
What was Zacchaeus saved from?

Luke addresses this in the parable, and we can see
it as long as we see where and how the system is
operative in the passage.

Many of us have struggled with this passage because
we see verse 26 as the spiritual takeaway of the
passage. "I tell you that to everyone who has, more
will be given, but as for the one who has nothing,
even what they have will be taken away." This is a
mistake. A plain reading of the text shows a very
different interpretation. By looking at the social
systems that Jesus describes in the passage, we can
unlock the meaning of the parable.

The first thing we notice is that the person with power
is a bad character. They are the villain of the story.
We know verse 26 is not the lesson because it is said
by a character that is meant to be the baddie. This is
an evil person that sets up an evil system.

First, this person specifically goes to another location,
sets himself up as the authority figure, and intends to
benefit from that place even as he is absent. This
parable may be roughly 1,492 years before
Christopher Columbus, but I cannot help but read the
colonization of Africa, South Asia, or the Americas in

a description like this. This person travels to a place not their own, takes power, sets up a system to benefit themselves at the expense of others, and intends to come back and reap the rewards.

To the surprise of no one, the people of that area do not want this person to be their king and are quite vocal about it. But this person of noble birth is successful. Wealth and power enable the injustice to happen. So he sets up a system where he gives ten minas to three people to invest in order to make him more money. There is no sense that this system was set up for anyone else's benefit but the king's. The text does not even indicate that the people who were to make the king this money were going to benefit from it themselves. This was an exploitive system from the beginning.

Two of the three people capitulate to the power and system. They assimilate to the colonizer's way. The first makes the king ten more minas. This person is rewarded for their participation in the evil system of the unjust king. They are given ten cities to rule over. Similarly, the person who made five minas is given five cities to rule over.

As people of color, there can be a real temptation to (and reward for) going along with unjust systems. We may swallow our critiques and pride to keep working at an organization that provides some level of material security. We may not confront that racism because making waves might cost us opportunity. We may even take part in perpetuating unjust systems like policing, housing, the military, etc. Sometimes it is tough to find ourselves operating at all outside of those systems. We all, by virtue of living in a society built to counter what we bring, are being exploited and are exploiting others.

These two servants, by choice or by force, capitulate to the terms given to them by the very person they never wanted to be ruled by. But the third servant is the hero of the story. We know this because they stand up to the system of an evil person. This is the person in the story that embodies the good. This is the example Jesus is calling upon in telling the story. Zacchaeus denounced an unjust system and it cost him more than half of his possessions. Jesus now tells this story to show another example of the cost of standing up to unjust systems.

The hero of the story did not do the king wrong. He gave him back his mina. Then he names the injustice of this powerful person. He tells him what everyone knows. The king delights to profit in ways that he does not deserve. Even through the hero's own fear, he names the wrong, to which the king agrees. The king does not even try to hide the fact that he enjoys his dishonest methods of gains.

This seems all too prevalent in today's US American landscape. A generation ago, it seemed that at least those who exploit others would hide or sugar coat it. It is now out in the open. It seems like overt racism is now back in vogue. I hear many people now subscribe to the philosophy, "When someone shows you who they are, you should believe them." Public officials, billionaire CEOs, and those who traffic in power are more and more emboldened to stand by their affection for injustice without any attempts at masking it.

This king owns his sin and thinks he is using the hero's own words against him, but really the brilliance of the parable is the character of the king using his words to show his evil. The king asks the hero why he did not just put the money in the bank to gain interest and benefit him at least a little bit. The king still misunderstands the hero and what makes him the hero. Our hero will do nothing to benefit the evil king, even at his own detriment. Our hero will play no part in any system designed to benefit the colonizer that has taken control of his community.

Power does not like to be confronted. Powerful people do not like their power to be usurped. The greatest offense to those that perpetuate evil power is the assurance that we can opt out of it. Power will always respond with rewarding itself and using violence to reinforce and provide retribution. The king becomes completely unhinged in response to the challenge to his power and the ability to opt out of his system.

His first act is to take the one mina and give it to the servant that has the ten. Others around object, but this makes complete sense from the vantage point of oppression and colonization. You will want to reward the servants most that most publicly surrender themselves to the ways of the system. To give the mina to the one with five is to help the person with five. To give the mina to the one with ten is to help the whole system of making dishonest wealth for the king. The king acts in his own greatest self-interest.

Then comes the most painful part of the story. It is the part of the story that we can also identify with the most. Standing up to the system will often not only have consequences upon you, but it will also have consequences on your whole community. The oppressors may target your family or your neighborhood if you get out of line with the system.

To show how unacceptable it was for the servant to stand up to the king and his system, the king then says in verse 26, "I tell you that to everyone who has, more will be given, but as for the one who has nothing, even what they have will be taken away." The king is so committed to his unjust system that he wants to reward even more those that submit to it by taking from the poor and giving to the rich. All of those that are willing to go along with the king's ways will be given more, which will be taken from those that have little.

This is the opposite of what Zacchaeus was doing. He was giving back to the people what the wealthy had taken from them. Therefore, Jesus declared that salvation had found his house. The parable is just a personification of what Zacchaeus had done. This is what Jesus is begging his followers who are from marginalized communities to do: stand up against the systems that are oppressing your people. He is also speaking truth to power, knowing that power is inevitably going to fight back.

The final verse of the story shows just how far the powerful will go to preserve their system. "But those enemies of mine who did not want me to be king over them—bring them here and kill them in front of me."

If the gospel is fundamentally about liberation, then the enemies of the gospel are about bondage. After this passage Jesus is headed to Jerusalem to die. He knows the pathway in front of him. In the story, things are about to get real. The first verse of the story is not an odd cryptic phase, "While they were listening to this, he went on to tell them a parable, because he was near Jerusalem and the people thought that the kingdom of God was going to appear at once."

Why this message of the cost of standing up to power to those who thought the kingdom of God would appear imminently?

While in many ways Zacchaeus represents the hero of the story, our task is to find ourselves in these stories. We are this man also. We live in a land with a system and power that is looking for us to be exploited for its own good. Our task is to stand up to power but be warned of the consequences of it. I am sure Zacchaeus could not have lasted in the tax collector community after giving back all that he had taken unjustly. I am pretty sure his professional union would kick him out. Jesus was warning Zacchaeus as he is warning us. As the kingdom of God is coming, stand up to the systems and structures that oppress, and be aware that injustice will not go down without a fight.

The Bible speaks to systems and structures in so many passages. As it does, our task is to be aware of how the system is functioning and consider what the right response is to that system.

Chapter 4
What is the Gospel?
Isaiah 61:1-6

The Spirit of the Sovereign Lord is on me,
  because the Lord has anointed me
  to proclaim good news to the poor.
He has sent me to bind up the brokenhearted,
  to proclaim freedom for the captives
  and release from darkness for the
prisoners,[a]
2 to proclaim the year of the Lord's favor
  and the day of vengeance of our God,
to comfort all who mourn,
3 and provide for those who grieve in Zion—
to bestow on them a crown of beauty
  instead of ashes,
the oil of joy
  instead of mourning,
and a garment of praise
  instead of a spirit of despair.
They will be called oaks of righteousness,
  a planting of the Lord
  for the display of his splendor.
4 They will rebuild the ancient ruins
  and restore the places long devastated;
they will renew the ruined cities
  that have been devastated for generations.
5 Strangers will shepherd your flocks;

foreigners will work your fields and
vineyards.
[6] And you will be called priests of the Lord,
you will be named ministers of our God.
You will feed on the wealth of nations,
and in their riches you will boast.

To this point we have examined how finding culture,
power, and systems in the scriptures help unlock the
liberative vantage point from which the scriptures are
written. This serves to help us find ourselves in the
story. Isaiah 61 gives us a peek into the foundations
of God's work in the world that we call the "gospel."
As the story of the church unfolds, the later writers of
the New Testament claim that false gospels will
spring up and plague the church. This is true in our
day as well, so we must be clear in what we think,
speak, and act on as the gospel.

The Gospel is not hidden in scriptures. God is not shy
about the priorities of the kingdom. The God of the
Hebrew scriptures and the Christian New Testament
is the God of the oppressed whose agenda is to lift up
those on the margins and bring down the people and
systems that oppress. Perhaps nowhere in the
scriptures is the heart of God shown better than in
Isaiah 61.

This has been a guiding light to me as I have navigated the promises of restoration and liberation in a world that constantly berates me with racism. After all, James Baldwin said, "To be a negro in this country and be relatively conscious is to be in a rage almost all the time." The scriptures are profoundly good news for the outsider, sick, poor, etc. You get a sense of a certain divine oversight from God in the scriptures. Those who have read the scriptures before us call it God's "preferential option for the poor." This passage beautifully makes a promise to those at the center of God's concern.

Remember our primary task is finding ourselves in the scriptures. Not everyone is the "you" from this passage. The "you" is the poor, the brokenhearted, the captive, and the prisoner. This is who the scripture is addressing. This is a particular "you," it is an intentional "you," and it is consistent with the heart of God throughout the scriptures. This is all of us in spaces where our relative consciousness cannot help but put us in a sort of rage almost all the time.

The first step that is poetically outlined by Isaiah is a divine healing. The systems of power and injustice bring real world trauma to those who live in subjection to them. Recent psychological research has found that trauma is also cultural and generational. The wages of sinful systems are death but God, in

Christ, offers liberation and new life.

Healing is closely followed by a divine authorization. It almost serves as a prerequisite according to Isaiah's poetry. Those who are the brokenhearted are healed so that they are the righteousness and planting of the Lord. The divine healing is first, but then makes a leap. God is building upon the healing with purpose. Not only will you be healed, but also you will receive a call. The call is connected to the healing and the healing empowers the call. This is a unique call for those that God has placed at the center of concern.

When I was 12 years old, my dad left my mom. A few weeks later, we received notice of a total eviction. I came home from school, our stuff was on the lawn, and I never entered my childhood house again. Everything flipped in one day. We were heartbroken and devastated. After a while, I accepted what God was doing with me and I healed from that space. It was then that I could walk into my call. I live the promise of these passages.

But what is the call that this scripture indicates? The text takes a turn after the call.

And *they*, who are the healed and called, shall rebuild the wasted cities. The healed and called will be the ones to raise cities that have been the object of injustice for many generations. The very cities that have oppressed our parents and grandparents need the renewing that only we can offer. Our cities, neighborhoods, and communities have been decimated by the sins of gentrification, mass incarceration, redlining, etc. Those who represent whiteness and majority culture cannot do justice in these spaces without the deep connection of black and brown people leading and contributing to the call. Even their best goodwill initiatives will fall short without marginalized people of color involved in their leadership. So God is raising up oppressed people to be leaders, find justice, and build. When structures are built that raise up the most vulnerable, everyone benefits.

Let's make it very contemporary with a poetic activity of our own:

"You who have been victims of lower wages,
        you will repair the systems of poverty.
You who experience racism,
        you will be the ones to build better communities for those who have been systematically disenfranchised.
You who have been told what you can and cannot do with your bodies,
        you will rebuild healthcare.
You who have been unjustly incarcerated,

you will reimagine policing and community safety.
You who have been targeted by child welfare services,
you will recreate community-based family systems of care."

I have pastored many people, old and young. I am amazed at how many of us wonder how to understand God's will for our life. While sometimes we get lost in the particulars, let me be clear with what I have come to understand. This healing and call are the will of God, for us to use the healing God has given us to "restore the places long devastated; they will renew the ruined cities."

Perhaps even literally.

In the colonized version of community building and rebuilding, it is the rich that do the work of deciding what the poor need. So many people in the name of faith have tried to "save those poor people and bring God to the city." I have been to many college chapels that even sing a particular song to this end. It is bad theology and a poor reading of scripture. God has said who his people are. They are not the powerful who want to make our cities in ways that benefit the wealthy. It is those that are committed to rebuild cities from the bottom up.

We have been enculturated to read scripture top-down, but that is backwards. The scriptures are for the healing, calling, and work of the marginalized for liberation and to remake the world into the kingdom of God. It is there, but we have been taught not to see it. We have not been taught to read God's word as God intends.

What does that mean for leaders and leadership? We are to rebuild unjust systems with just ones. We are to build opportunity where dead ends exist. The call to reclaim a city is a call to form different types of systems like healthcare, transportation, childcare, education, economics. Our cities need us. No one else can do it.

Most major movements start with young people. I saw this firsthand in Ferguson, Missouri after Mike Brown was murdered in the streets by police officers. As I landed in Ferguson expecting to help the moment, it became clear that the work in that community would need to be driven by younger activists. Black Lives Matter is a young person's movement. I saw clearly that their leadership was not just from their learning and experience but was the result of a promise from the Creator. You have what it takes because God has said so. There cannot be any imposter syndrome when God has set the ways of leadership in motion. We do not need white metrics and white affirmations when we have the scriptures. Even Paul in the New Testament had problems with his own leadership and God's credentialing him, but he lived into his leadership based upon God's commission.

There is a promise of promotion and reparation. God says:

"Here is a little extra for your shame you have had to live under.
    You will receive double.
For all the stuff you have had to do that is two times more than the white people,
    you will receive more from me.
For women who have had to do three times more than their male colleagues,
    you receive more.
For all of the back-breaking,
    you will receive double."

What is the double? What is the blessing of God? It is family, culture, your spouse, doors opening, people, or greater influence. This is God's justice, "because you went through that, I will double up some things in your life."

White systems and culture will tell you that you

should be grateful for what has been given to you within systems that marginalize you. This is dangerous and antithetical to the gospel. I have experienced this over and over when religious denominations or nonprofit organizations want to finally invest in people of color. We are given a fraction of what is spent on white initiatives and we are expected to respond with a posture of thankfulness to these white interest masters. As if they want to overlook the work we have done to get to where we are and the history of systemic marginalization their affiliations have on our communities.

In the Netflix series *All American,* a Black player is before his white coach during a conflict. As it gets heated the coach says, "You should be grateful and show more respect." The assumption is that the player needs someone who is white to give him the opportunity to play. What is more truthful is that he worked his ass off by working in the gym, being committed to the weight room, and learning his sport. No white person got him to that space. No white people have gotten us into ours, even if we have met a few in our journey that have been on our side.

You put in the work with your lives, vocations, careers, skills, and passions. This is why you have endured. This is why your leadership is strong.

We live in a country where power and money dictate so much opportunity, social capital, reputation, and advancement. This is not the same all over the world. Many places are not built in that manner. God does not work on those terms. I have witnessed places and moments where God shows up from nothing. Where miracles look and feel like the ones we read about in the scriptures. This is the God of the Hebrew scriptures and the Christian New Testament that is centering the work of the kingdom upon the marginalized

It may be challenging to be comfortable in what the liberation of the scriptures brings to us. It may not seem true because it is so counter to what western white culture brings to us. We spend so much time wrestling with what is true about us. We measure the liberation of the God of the scriptures against the backdrop of white theology and miss the truth of Isaiah 61.

I sit with groups regularly and ask the provocative question, "Who gave white people the power to be the framers of theology for the world?" It was not the God of these scriptures. Dominant culture has mastered the art of controlling the narrative. It is true of history, it is true of the social dynamics of today, and it is true of much of the contemporary outgrowth of historic Christianity.

What we do is snatch it back.

In my religious upbringing and education, I had so many questions but didn't have the safe and brave space to ask them. I had questions that contested assumptions and disputed what I had been taught, and ultimately led me to liberation. So often I let it go, but I kept reading the scriptures.

In one instance at Bible school, I had a teacher that was teaching capital punishment as God's way that we should want to vote for and form our society around. I knew in my spirit that this was wrong, but I didn't have all of the tools to push against it. From that point I knew that part of my vocation was to first learn the tools to challenge interpretations of scripture that I felt were wrong, then pass along those tools to others. As I found out, the tools are rooted in the scriptures themselves. They are the gospel. They are liberation.

Jesus using Isaiah 61

Many have suggested that Luke 4 contains Jesus' mission statement. We postulate that, in Jesus' time, when Jesus quotes a small amount of scripture, the audience assumes he is referencing the larger idea. In

Luke 4, he quotes this passage:

> [14] Jesus returned to Galilee in the power of the Spirit, and news about him spread through the whole countryside. [15] He was teaching in their synagogues, and everyone praised him.

> [16] He went to Nazareth, where he had been brought up, and on the Sabbath day he went into the synagogue, as was his custom. He stood up to read, [17] and the scroll of the prophet Isaiah was handed to him. Unrolling it, he found the place where it is written:

> [18] "The Spirit of the Lord is on me,
>   because he has anointed me
>   to proclaim good news to the poor.
> He has sent me to proclaim freedom for the prisoners
>   and recovery of sight for the blind,
> to set the oppressed free,
> [19] to proclaim the year of the Lord's favor."

> [20] Then he rolled up the scroll, gave it back to the attendant and sat down. The eyes of everyone in the synagogue were fastened on him. [21] He began by saying to them, "Today this scripture is fulfilled in your hearing."

> [22] All spoke well of him and were amazed at the gracious words that came from his lips.

"Isn't this Joseph's son?" they asked.

23 Jesus said to them, "Surely you will quote this proverb to me: 'Physician, heal yourself!' And you will tell me, 'Do here in your hometown what we have heard that you did in Capernaum.'"

24 "Truly I tell you," he continued, "no prophet is accepted in his hometown. 25 I assure you that there were many widows in Israel in Elijah's time, when the sky was shut for three and a half years and there was a severe famine throughout the land. 26 Yet Elijah was not sent to any of them, but to a widow in Zarephath in the region of Sidon. 27 And there were many in Israel with leprosy in the time of Elisha the prophet, yet not one of them was cleansed—only Naaman the Syrian."

28 All the people in the synagogue were furious when they heard this. 29 They got up, drove him out of the town, and took him to the brow of the hill on which the town was built, in order to throw him off the cliff. 30 But he walked right through the crowd and went on his way.

This passage shows the danger of the elite interpreting scriptures that are not meant for them.

Jesus participates in the religious duty by reading the scroll with Isaiah 61 on it. Everyone commends him for reading, not realizing that they are not the object of this good news. He foretells his betrayal because he knows what he is about to say next will stir up the elite crowd against him. He is faced with the challenge of communicating the gospel as God intends and that Isaiah poetically communicates. This gospel is that the marginalized are healed, called, and will rebuild broken cities and social structures that once marginalized them. That even applies to religious systems.

But this audience is not the marginalized. This group has power over the religious system of the day. They create the language, rhythms, and theologies about who is in and who is out. We know from later in the gospels that there were systems of exploitation in the religion that Jesus was born into. Jesus was commended for speaking the religious text. He was condemned when he applied it to the powerful of his day. It reminds us of the quote from Dom Hélder Câmara, Archbishop of Brazil in the 20th century: "When I feed the poor, they call me a saint, but when I ask why the poor are hungry, they call me a communist."

Jesus calls upon another story of the scriptures from 2 Kings 5. Jesus tells them that God has chosen to work outside of their religious system in the time of cultural religious heroes. For three and a half years, there was a famine in the land and there was an outbreak of leprosy. The God of the Hebrew people did not send their prophet Elisha to one of their own people with leprosy, but to one of the Syrians - the captain in the Syrian King's army. God skipped over his own people.

Similarly, Jesus is saying that God is skipping over them and claiming this gospel is not for his own people but for those outside. The gospel is for those not born into the right elite family, those outside of the social hierarchy, those that did not have the ability to pay the right religious taxes, those who came from the wrong ancestry. This is what we find through the duration of the book of Luke. All of these folks are lifted up as examples of faithfulness in the face of those who claim to have authority over how God operates in the world.

Those who resist power being handed to the marginalized are predictable in their responses. Like the unjust king in the parable, these folks responded with violence. This is a path we know altogether too well. They go from marveling at Jesus' words to trying to throw him off a cliff. They did not seek to understand him and the error of their ways. They were not in a position of learning. They were not interested in being curious. Power uses violence to assert its dominance in the face of those that challenge it. We see this on the streets of our cities and in the capitals of many countries that oppress their people.

This passage is seen by many as Jesus' mission statement because his actions from here on out prove it. Jesus, tempted with power and compromise, stays true to his assertion that the gospel of healing, calling, and rebuilding is centrally for those on the margins. If you have not spent much time reading the Bible, I challenge you to read the rest of the book of Luke with this in mind.

As we do, we will see that fault lines are drawn by culture, systems, and power. As we live lives negotiating US American life, western cultural values, and the contemporary versions of Christianity, we find our place in the story and before God as people who are healing, though that can be slow and look like many things; called, though that is broader than our religious traditions have taught us; and rebuilding in ways that often scare the elite towards aggression and violence.

Chapter 5
Healing and Calling
John 4: 1-42

Now Jesus learned that the Pharisees had heard that he was gaining and baptizing more disciples than John - although in fact it was not Jesus who baptized, but his disciples. ³ So he left Judea and went back once more to Galilee.

⁴ Now he had to go through Samaria. ⁵ So he came to a town in Samaria called Sychar, near the plot of ground Jacob had given to his son Joseph. ⁶ Jacob's well was there, and Jesus, tired as he was from the journey, sat down by the well. It was about noon.

⁷ When a Samaritan woman came to draw water, Jesus said to her, "Will you give me a drink?" ⁸ (His disciples had gone into the town to buy food.)

⁹ The Samaritan woman said to him, "You are a Jew and I am a Samaritan woman. How can you ask me for a drink?" (For Jews do not associate with Samaritans.[a])

¹⁰ Jesus answered her, "If you knew the gift of God and who it is that asks you for a drink, you would have asked him and he would have given you living water."

¹¹ "Sir," the woman said, "you have nothing to

draw with and the well is deep. Where can you get this living water?¹² Are you greater than our father Jacob, who gave us the well and drank from it himself, as did also his sons and his livestock?"

¹³ Jesus answered, "Everyone who drinks this water will be thirsty again, ¹⁴ but whoever drinks the water I give them will never thirst. Indeed, the water I give them will become in them a spring of water welling up to eternal life."

¹⁵ The woman said to him, "Sir, give me this water so that I won't get thirsty and have to keep coming here to draw water."

¹⁶ He told her, "Go, call your husband and come back."

¹⁷ "I have no husband," she replied.

Jesus said to her, "You are right when you say you have no husband. ¹⁸ The fact is, you have had five husbands, and the man you now have is not your husband. What you have just said is quite true."

¹⁹ "Sir," the woman said, "I can see that you are a prophet. ²⁰ Our ancestors worshiped on this mountain, but you Jews claim that the place where we must worship is in Jerusalem."

²¹ "Woman," Jesus replied, "believe me, a time is coming when you will worship the

Father neither on this mountain nor in Jerusalem. ²² You Samaritans worship what you do not know; we worship what we do know, for salvation is from the Jews. ²³ Yet a time is coming and has now come when the true worshipers will worship the Father in the Spirit and in truth, for they are the kind of worshipers the Father seeks. ²⁴ God is spirit, and his worshipers must worship in the Spirit and in truth."

²⁵ The woman said, "I know that Messiah" (called Christ) "is coming. When he comes, he will explain everything to us."

²⁶ Then Jesus declared, "I, the one speaking to you—I am he."

The Disciples Rejoin Jesus

²⁷ Just then his disciples returned and were surprised to find him talking with a woman. But no one asked, "What do you want?" or "Why are you talking with her?"

²⁸ Then, leaving her water jar, the woman went back to the town and said to the people, ²⁹ "Come, see a man who told me everything I ever did. Could this be the Messiah?" ³⁰ They came out of the town and made their way toward him.

³¹ Meanwhile his disciples urged him, "Rabbi, eat something."

³² But he said to them, "I have food to eat that you know nothing about."

³³ Then his disciples said to each other, "Could someone have brought him food?"

³⁴ "My food," said Jesus, "is to do the will of him who sent me and to finish his work. ³⁵ Don't you have a saying, 'It's still four months until harvest'? I tell you, open your eyes and look at the fields! They are ripe for harvest. ³⁶ Even now the one who reaps draws a wage and harvests a crop for eternal life, so that the sower and the reaper may be glad together. ³⁷ Thus the saying 'One sows and another reaps' is true. ³⁸ I sent you to reap what you have not worked for. Others have done the hard work, and you have reaped the benefits of their labor."

Many Samaritans Believe

³⁹ Many of the Samaritans from that town believed in him because of the woman's testimony, "He told me everything I ever did." ⁴⁰ So when the Samaritans came to him, they urged him to stay with them, and he stayed two days. ⁴¹ And because of his words many more became believers.

⁴² They said to the woman, "We no longer believe just because of what you said; now we have heard for ourselves, and we know that

this man really is the Savior of the world."

Culture and system come together in the interpretation of the story of the Samaritan woman. This incredible story shows the Isaiah 61 pattern of the gospel of healing, calling, and rebuilding from someone on the margins. As we have been tasked to find ourselves in the story, we are challenged anew by this one as even the disciples, those closest to the ministry of the gospel, missed where the work was. All the while Jesus clearly saw the person who would change the community that had ostracized her.

The story begins with the religious pastors and theologians of their day seeing Jesus as competition. Jesus seemed uninterested in their game of counting numbers of religious converts. Instead, he left the area and avoided this game of comparison. Here the geography tells the cultural story. Jesus was traveling from one city to another and in the process had to travel through an area with another cultural group. It was common practice for Jesus' people to have taken extra time to travel the long way around the area. This is familiar to us. Many of us come from neighborhoods that others avoid because they are deemed "not safe." Often, we carry those neighborhoods with us as we see dominant culture people lock their car doors when we walk by or change sides of the street when we approach them on the sidewalk. This dynamic of avoiding the cultural other has been around as long as there have been clashing civilizations.

But Jesus decides not to go around; instead, he goes straight through the undesirable neighborhood. He goes straight through culture.

Why were the Samaritans "othered" by the Jewish people? It goes back generations. It was because of their cultural heritage. They were seen as half-breeds compared to their pure-blooded Jewish neighbors. In the fictional wizarding world of Harry Potter, they are called "mudbloods." They are wizards with nonmagical muggle ancestry. So, the entire culture is looked down upon. We read this and see the parallels clearly to our time. Black people have been labeled as lazy or criminal even as we have built this country. Our Latinx siblings have been sinfully classified as rapists and murders. We know the stigmas that our country places on us. We know the conversations that go on about our neighborhoods and communities.

The disciples expect Jesus to take the road around the 'hood that was common to their lives. They expected him to take part in the common cultural ritual of dehumanizing the Samaritan people based upon cultural heritage. Isn't it interesting that the road chosen to travel spoke volumes to and contributed to the dehumanization of people? But this would be inconsistent with who Jesus is and the liberation he brings.

The liberating piece of this story is quite fascinating and follows the gospel of Isaiah 61 and Luke 4 so clearly.

Jesus shows up at a well in Samaria, tired from the journey, and encounters a woman there. The disciples are not with him and the story records no other people. It is commonly understood that the woman was probably there alone in the middle of the day because she was ostracized from her own community. Typically, a gathering of women going to the well would have happened early in the day in community for safety and to avoid the heat of the day. This woman is by herself, signaling a particular relationship with her community.

Jesus sees her as an important appointment he needs to get to. There is intentionality in going to Samaria. Jesus wants to bring a liberating message to the community of "half-breeds", and she is the perfect person. He engages her, centering her dignity rather than seeing her as a charity case.

The first thing Jesus does is ask her for a drink. He doesn't set himself up as the one helping her but he identifies his own need. This centers what she can contribute. This is an immediate identification of her humanity. She has something to give that is valuable. This is profound in light of what she means to her society. This is also something I learned through my relationship with CCDA and Dr. Perkins' teaching on this text. Jesus affirmed her *dignity* to begin the relationship, not her *need*.

She responds immediately from her place of internalized oppression. She knows how she is defined. She knows her place in the cultural hierarchy. Jesus and the woman have no specific conflict, yet there is instant tension. She names all the stereotypes and the human understandings of where she belongs. She repeats what has been told to her all of her life:

You are nothing.
You are less than a man.
Jews are better than you.

She has rehearsed it in her head and she repeats it to Jesus in this one statement: "You are a Jew and I am a Samaritan woman. How can you ask me for a drink?"

I know so many people of color who will let you know that they are seen as less than their white counterparts. They feel it deeply because of being treated as less. Over time we subsequently begin believing it. This is the psychology of oppression that we are bombarded with daily. The woman at the well names it for all of us who have felt this way.

We worked with a lot of kids when I lived in Atlanta. It is the greatest of heartbreaks hearing some of the ways black children internalize the messages from society. I heard statements like, "Graduating school and going to college is for white folks, not us," and "Well, do black people get married?" They could tell you their place in society, where they could go and not go, and what the expectation was for them. It is baked into the experience of growing up black in America, even in a city known for its incredible civil rights accomplishments. The oppression was voiced through the hearts of many of the young people living there.

Jesus immediately debunks the Samaritan woman's rehearsal of her place in society saying, "If you knew who I was – you would ask for a drink and never thirst again." If she could see and really know the heart of God, she would see her dignity, value, and worth.

Let's pause to remember the context. Jesus left a scene of competition over baptism numbers. God had no interest in the other scene, but the primary interest was in meeting this woman. What profound implications there are if we really take this seriously. If we put off the ways organized religion measures success and center the Isaiah 61 gospel of healing, calling, and renewing cities and systems, we might find ourselves right with the Samaritan women in our time, asking if we could get a drink of water from them.

Jesus indicates that if she understood this living water, she would be drinking it and never thirsting. What is that living water? Jesus offers to give her something that would teach her to never see herself that way ever again. That is pure gospel. Jesus left the leaders to be with her and indicates to her that she will never thirst again for what society has defined her as!

Can you imagine if oppressed folks, women in our time, and black indigenous people of color truly understood our value and call? Could you imagine if this message got through today? What if all of us that have internalized this crap all of our lives could never thirst for it again!

Jesus sets the record straight and she is in. She says, "Ok, give me this thing." The script gets flipped.

If you knew what was happening you would be the one asking for living water. Drinking living water represents that you are made special. Drinking living water represents that you are a daughter of God. Drinking living water represents that you can take away the stain of what society has done to you.

To illustrate this point Jesus then drops this line, "Go call your husband." This is where culture meets system. This is where all the shit breaks out.

She says, "I don't have any husband." But Jesus gives her more detail about her own life in saying that she has had multiple husbands and the man she is with now she is not married to. So many people get this part of the passage wrong because they refuse to look at how patriarchal systems are at play in the scriptures. If you have heard this passage before, you have probably heard people attribute her marital status to some sort of sin on her part. That is the wrong interpretation. I have heard her referred to as a "loose" woman. That is kind for "promiscuous behavior" that means she has been unfaithful to her husbands. All of this is simply an inability to see where systems are at play in the text.

Jesus is about to free this woman!

In that time in society, no woman ever decided to leave a man. It was impossible, unheard of, not an option. No woman was ever going to leave a husband for a second husband. Then leave a second for a third, then a third for a fourth because she felt like it. That is hogwash! The way patriarchy existed in that day was that she was essentially the property of these men until a time when they no longer wanted her.

She was thrown away five times. She may have even be given from one man to another. She never chose to leave; she was likely thrown out. When Jesus makes this statement to her, it is not an accusatory one, it is compassionate. In essence Jesus says, "I know you have been used and thrown away. I know you have been the victim of misogyny. I am freeing you from that, you will not need that from here on out." Jesus is saying whatever that has led you to believe about yourself, that is over. I thank Rev. Traci Blackmon for illuminating this point for me somewhere in our journeys together.

He liberates her - not her individual sin, but the societal sin that has used her and discarded her. Sinful systems will always dehumanize some for the benefit of others. Sinful systems are built on versions of superiority that indicate some are less than human and need to be treated as property. The scriptures teach that every human ever born in every culture and part of the world are made in the image of God, fearfully and wonderfully made, and deserving of reverence and respect.

Jesus was in that moment with that woman on purpose to let her know that she mattered even as she had been used by society. So many people need that same affirmation in our day.

Next, they get into a dialog about proper worship of the God who wants to liberate her from these societal systems of exploitation and cultural inferiority. This part can get a bit esoteric. Essentially Jesus breaks down their false religious expressions. What matters is the heart we bring to God. Not where we come from, not credentials, ordination, or education. It is not our place in flawed religious systems. We worship God in Spirit and in truth.

The disciples come back and she leaves. The scripture makes a point to say that she forgot her pot for getting water. This is a great metaphor, because she got what she needed and was no longer thirsty. She was healed, she was called, her next step is to go back to her city to rebuild. She went back to preach the gospel with a message of, "Come meet a man who told me everything about myself." Jesus knew all that she was and ordained her for leadership back to the community that ostracized her.

Jesus lifted this woman into leadership. It was such a powerful and prophetic move that he had to stay later than he intended. The reality of the change from the outcast to the leader is a smack in the face of those at the beginning of the story who were measuring leadership competitions about who was baptizing more people. By the end of the story, we know who a real leader is, and where real leadership really comes from.

In our day, labels that are given to black students by teachers early on still impact them into their high school years, if they make it that far. We are this woman because we fall into societal normative frameworks of who we are. It is remarkable how long internalized racism and colorism have been around. We are still seeing it to this day and it's been around since Biblical times. We all know that if someone is told something long enough, eventually they will start believing it.

The systems of injustice are built on the necessity of us internalizing our racism. For-profit prisons do their long-term budget projections based upon the reading level of third graders in marginalized communities. The system is built to determine a person's destiny by third grade in an education system not built for them.

The Samaritan woman went back and started preaching this liberation thing. Later in that chapter the disciples come back and they are absolutely clueless as to what is going on. There is a lesson on this as well. The woman has experienced life change and freedom, and the people who are closest to Jesus should have seen it but missed it. There is some internal work we need to do. Every person of color may not get it. She was not deterred going about the work of freedom because she is free.

She is free, having gone through a transformation, but it did not stop her from going to her own folks with the message. As people of color, we find ourselves throughout our education or other transformative processes going back into our communities that may not understand. We need our confidence built up to stay engaged with those in communities that we come from. Our growth and change are not a reason to abandon our communities. I have heard so many stories of people of color that cannot go back into their communities because of the emotional and relational cost of their transformation.

Don't let the haters keep you from taking your transformation back to your own folks. This may be the most important place for your transformation to be on display.

For marginalized folks, we are always talked about by
the worst part of our culture. We are ill-defined
by our struggles and the worst parts
of our marginalization. But we are fearfully and
wonderfully made, part of God's majesty, and chosen
for leadership.

The Great Commission

Matthew 28:16-20

> [16]Then the eleven disciples went to Galilee, to
> the mountain where Jesus had told them to
> go. [17]When they saw him, they worshiped
> him; but some doubted. [18]Then Jesus came to
> them and said, "All authority in heaven and on
> earth has been given to me. [19]Therefore go
> and make disciples of all nations, baptizing
> them in the name of the Father and of the Son
> and of the Holy Spirit, [20]and teaching them to
> obey everything I have commanded you. And
> surely I am with you always, to the very end
> of the age."

This scripture is a familiar one to many who have
been around church. It's considered the "great
commission" - the final words of Jesus to his

disciples before he is taken to heaven. These are the last words of direction to those around Jesus, and are seen as the great mission of the church to take this message of Jesus to all the world.

The disciples are gathered and suddenly Jesus appears to them. Some of the disciples begin to worship, but others doubt. The doubt is interesting as it speaks to where some of the closest followers find themselves after they watch a crucifixion, and even though they see Jesus risen, the doubts still hang in the air.

Jesus then gives the direction to go out and make disciples by sharing their stories. Go out and let people know of the work of the trinity and how it is manifested in the world. He reiterates: teach them about all I have taught you. And I am with you.

This is a powerful piece of scripture in my opinion, especially when you bring in the liberation aspect, which is the view from the margins. A view from the margins helps me understand the doubters even more.

You see, many have been taught a colonized view of this scripture. We have been taught to see it from a privileged point of view that this commission is for wealthy, privileged, and powerful people to take the message to poor and marginalized people. For example, the US taking the gospel to parts of Africa or "unreached" people groups. This is the complete opposite of what is happening contextually.

Jesus is not talking to privileged or powerful people; he is talking to people living on the edge of empire because of their affiliation with him or their place as "unlearned fishermen" (referring to Peter on one occasion in Acts). They were not the wealthy taking a message to the poor. They were the marginalized to whom Jesus was saying, "Go tell your story." I can see the doubters saying, but they killed you! What do you think they will do to us? I can imagine the doubters wondering, how in the world will we stand up to the power of Rome and the religious leaders?

Jesus answers the doubters by saying, "I am with you." Jesus talks directly to marginalized people, letting them know he walks with them and will be walking with them to the very end.

Jesus tells the marginalized folks I got you, I am with you, go tell your story. This is in direct contrast to the messages we may have heard.

Be liberated by the actions and words of Jesus to bring life and hope as he promises to the margins, "I am with you until the end."

About the Authors

Leroy Barber has dedicated 30 years living and working towards what Dr. King called "the beloved community."

Leroy starts projects that shape society. In 1989, burdened by the plight of Philadelphia's homeless, he and his wife, Donna, founded Restoration Ministries to serve homeless families and children living on the streets. In 1994 he became Director of Internship Programs at Cornerstone Christian Academy. Leroy was licensed and ordained at Mt Zion Baptist Church where he served as Youth Director with Donna, and also served as Associate Minister of Evangelism. In 1997 he joined FCS Urban Ministries in Atlanta, GA working with the Atlanta Youth Project to serve as the founding Executive Director of Atlanta Youth Academies, a private elementary school providing quality Christian education for low-income families in the inner city. Leroy also helped found DOOR Atlanta, Community Life Church, South Atlanta Marketplace, and Community Grounds Coffee shop in Atlanta, as well as Green My Hood and The Voices Project. Leroy is an innovator, entrepreneur and lover of the arts. Leroy has a Masters Degree in Divinity and a D. Min.

Leroy is the Executive Director of Neighborhood

Economics, the Co-Founder of the Voices Project, and Adjunct professor at Multnomah University. He has served on the boards of The Simple Way, Missio Alliance, The Evangelical Environmental Network (EEN), and is the Former Board Chair of the Christian Community Development Association (CCDA).

Jess Bielman has successfully become a pastoral presence for a generation of people who have said "no" to pastors in a traditional sense. He is a mentor to those who minister in the name of Jesus to a church that historically has not valued their perspectives. Jess prepares leaders to engage community in ways that honor the dignity of all people and cultures.
He has been mentored and engaged leaders in cultural work and developed initiatives that center the voices on the margins. He has worked with scholars and practitioners to co-constructed programs, curriculum, and content that analyzes theological and cultural issues impacting the thriving of church and community.
A Northwest native who converted to the Christian faith as a teenager, Jess has long been interested in the intersection faith community and local culture. These interests have driven his personal explorations, ecclesial life, and academic interests. Jess is always looking to discover the next iteration of the church in the world

Jess earned his doctorate in ministry with a dissertation exploring contextualizing ministry training to the Pacific Northwest. As a college professor, he has taught bible, historic Christian spirituality, faith and culture, community engagement, and preaching, among other subjects. Jess has developed programs and curriculum to train pastors and students to engage in ministry at the margins of cities, neighborhoods, and society.

Jess is an ordained minister and pastor by calling who has done campus ministry and house church ministry. As a campus pastor he oversaw the evolution of ministry programs to a religiously and culturally diverse college campus always looking toward meeting the needs of students. He is a trusted partner with those who are navigating 'dark night of the soul' experiences and other faith transitions.

Jess is a skilled administrator having worked on strategic planning, systems and structure change, and creative initiative implementation. He is an innovator committed to changing institutional culture to enact more equitable processes. Jess has often been called upon to rethink and restructure systems designed to serve the core values of the organization.

Made in USA - Kendallville, IN
46808_9798375532998
02.09.2023 1321